JEREMY SULLIVAN

WHISPERS
OF THE
WORD
A COLLECTION OF BIBLE VERSE POEMS

★

YOUAREAGOODPERSON.COM

This is for every voice hoping for better days, every dreamer reaching high, and the gentle, calm souls whose quiet hands guide and cheer us on.

—good times

TABLE OF CONTENTS

PATH OF FAITH AND LIFE

God, our source, through Jesus Christ, our guide,
Calls us to Faith, from Sin to Salvation,
Through Love, He gives the Law and Covenant,
And in Prayer, we find Prophecy fulfilled.

The Kingdom of God brings Righteousness near,
Forgiveness frees us from Judgment's weight,
In Worship we rise, filled with the Holy Spirit,
As the Church is bound in His endless Grace.

The Gospel speaks of the Law and Commandments,
And through Suffering, Wisdom is born,
Eternal Life waits for Obedient hearts,
And in Hope, we stand, faithful and strong.

Justice and Humility shape our path,
Joy and Peace fill us, Patience guides,
Kindness and Self-Control lift us higher,
Faithfulness and Mercy sustain us through trials.

Strength flows within us, Courage leads on,
With Perseverance and Spiritual Gifts in hand,
Repentance brings Holiness, Truth lights our way,
Creation sings of Miracles around us.

In Parables of Jesus, Healing abounds,
God's Promises hold true each day,
The Fear of the Lord draws us together in Unity,
And Generosity binds us, now and always.

A JOURNEY OF FAITH

God, in Jesus Christ, brings Faith to life,
Calling us to turn from Sin to Salvation,
Guided by Love and the Law, bound in Covenant,
We lift our Prayer, and through Prophecy, find hope.

In the Kingdom of God, we seek Righteousness,
Receiving Forgiveness and fearing Judgment no more,
Our Worship rises, touched by the Holy Spirit,
As the Church unites, embraced by Grace.

The Gospel of truth fulfills the Law and Commandments,
Turning our Suffering into Wisdom gained,
And Eternal Life awaits the Obedient heart,
For Hope endures through Stewardship and giving.

With Justice and Humility, we walk in Joy and Peace,
Bearing Patience, Kindness, and Self-Control,
Faithfulness lights the way, as Mercy guides us,
Strength fills our souls, giving Courage to endure.

Perseverance shapes us, through Spiritual Gifts bestowed,
Repentance brings Holiness, and Truth becomes our guide,
Creation sings, Miracles abound,
In Parables of Jesus, Healing flows.

God's Promises hold us; in the Fear of the Lord, we stand,
Bound in Unity, we live Generosity each day,
From the beginning to the end,
God is with us—our Guide, our Strength, our All.

FOUNDATION OF FAITH

lay the doctrinal ground first

GOD

The Creator's Power

"In the beginning, God created the heavens and the earth."

"The earth is the Lord's, and everything in it,
The world, and all who live in it."

"For He spoke, and it came to be;
He commanded, and it stood firm."

Genesis 1:1; Psalm 24:1; Psalm 33:9

God's Everlasting Love

"The Lord is compassionate and gracious,
Slow to anger, abounding in love."

"Give thanks to the Lord, for He is good;
His love endures forever."

"For the mountains may depart and the hills be removed,
But my steadfast love shall not depart from you."

Psalm 103:8; Psalm 136:1; Isaiah 54:10

The Lord, My Strength

"The Lord is my strength and my shield;
My heart trusts in Him, and He helps me."

"God is our refuge and strength,
An ever-present help in trouble."

"My flesh and my heart may fail,
But God is the strength of my heart and my portion forever."

Psalm 28:7; Psalm 46:1; Psalm 73:26

The Almighty's Wisdom

"Great is our Lord and mighty in power;
His understanding has no limit."

"If any of you lacks wisdom, you should ask God,
Who gives generously to all without finding fault, and it
will be given to you."

"Oh, the depth of the riches of the wisdom and knowledge
of God!"

Psalm 147:5; James 1:5; Romans 11:33

God's Faithfulness

"The Lord is faithful to all His promises
And loving toward all He has made."

"Because of the Lord's great love, we are not consumed,
For His compassions never fail.
They are new every morning;
Great is Your faithfulness."

"Know therefore that the Lord Your God is God;
He is the faithful God, keeping His covenant of love."

Psalm 145:13; Lamentations 3:22-23; Deuteronomy 7:9

Thoughts & Prayer

JESUS CHRIST

The Way, the Truth, and the Life

"Jesus answered, 'I am the way and the truth and the life. No one comes to the Father except through me.'"

"For there is one God and one mediator between God and mankind, The man Christ Jesus."

"Salvation is found in no one else, For there is no other name under heaven given to mankind by which we must be saved."

John 14:6; 1 Timothy 2:5; Acts 4:12

The Light of the World

"When Jesus spoke again to the people, He said, 'I am the light of the world.

Whoever follows me will never walk in darkness, But will have the light of life.'"

"For you were once darkness, but now you are light in the Lord.

Live as children of light."

John 8:12; Ephesians 5:8

The Good Shepherd

"I am the good shepherd.
The good shepherd lays down His life for the sheep."

"My sheep listen to my voice;
I know them, and they follow me."

"I give them eternal life, and they shall never perish;
No one will snatch them out of my hand."

John 10:11, John 10:27-28

The Lamb of God

"Look, the Lamb of God,
Who takes away the sin of the world!"

"He was led like a lamb to the slaughter,
And as a sheep before its shearers is silent,
So He did not open His mouth."

"For Christ, our Passover lamb, has been sacrificed."

John 1:29; Isaiah 53:7; 1 Corinthians 5:7

The Resurrection and the Life

"Jesus said to her, 'I am the resurrection and the life.
The one who believes in me will live,
Even though they die; And whoever lives by believing in
me will never die.'"

"For as in Adam all die, so in Christ all will be made alive."

John 11:25-26; 1 Corinthians 15:22

Thoughts & Prayer

THE HOLY SPIRIT

The Helper

"And I will ask the Father, and He will give you another Helper,
To be with you forever, the Spirit of truth."

"But the Helper, the Holy Spirit,
Whom the Father will send in my name,
He will teach you all things."

John 14:16-17; John 14:26

The Spirit of God Dwells in You

"Do you not know that you are God's temple
And that God's Spirit dwells in you?"

"But if Christ is in you, even though your body is subject to death
because of sin,

The Spirit gives life because of righteousness."

1 Corinthians 3:16; Romans 8:10

Led by the Spirit

"For those who are led by the Spirit of God
Are the children of God."

"So I say, walk by the Spirit,
And you will not gratify the desires of the flesh."

Romans 8:14; Galatians 5:16

The Fruits of the Spirit

"But the fruit of the Spirit is love, joy, peace,
Forbearance, kindness, goodness, faithfulness, gentleness
and self-control."

"Since we live by the Spirit,
Let us keep in step with the Spirit."

Galatians 5:22-23; Galatians 5:25

Power of the Holy Spirit

"But you will receive power when the Holy Spirit comes on you;

And you will be my witnesses in Jerusalem, and in all Judea and Samaria,
And to the ends of the earth."

"Now the Lord is the Spirit, and where the Spirit of the Lord is, there is freedom."

Acts 1:8; 2 Corinthians 3:17

Thoughts & Prayer

THE GOSPEL

The Good News

"For I am not ashamed of the gospel,
Because it is the power of God that brings salvation
To everyone who believes."

"Go into all the world and preach the gospel to all
creation."

Romans 1:16; Mark 16:15

The Message of the Cross

"For the message of the cross is foolishness to those who
are perishing,

But to us who are being saved it is the power of God."

"We preach Christ crucified: a stumbling block to Jews
And foolishness to Gentiles."

1 Corinthians 1:18; 1 Corinthians 1:23

Christ Died for Us

"As it is written: 'How beautiful are the feet
Of those who bring good news!'"

"And with your feet fitted with the readiness
That comes from the gospel of peace."

Romans 10:15; Ephesians 6:15

The Gospel of Peace

"But God demonstrates His own love for us in this:
While we were still sinners, Christ died for us."

"For what I received I passed on to you as of first importance:
That Christ died for our sins according to the Scriptures,
That He was buried, that He was raised on the third day."

Romans 5:8; 1 Corinthians 15:3-4

The Power of the Gospel

"For the grace of God has appeared
That offers salvation to all people."

"This gospel of the kingdom will be preached in the whole
world

As a testimony to all nations, and then the end will come."

Titus 2:11; Matthew 24:14

Thoughts & Prayer

SALVATION

Salvation by Grace

"For it is by grace you have been saved, through faith—
And this is not from yourselves, it is the gift of God—
Not by works, so that no one can boast."

"God saved us, not because of righteous things we had done,

But because of His mercy."

Ephesians 2:8-9; Titus 3:5

Believe and Be Saved

"If you declare with your mouth, 'Jesus is Lord,'
And believe in your heart that God raised Him from the dead,

You will be saved."

"Everyone who calls on the name of the Lord will be saved."

Romans 10:9; Romans 10:13

The Lord is My Salvation

"The Lord is my light and my salvation—whom shall I fear?
The Lord is the stronghold of my life—of whom shall I be
afraid?"

"Surely God is my salvation; I will trust and not be afraid.
The Lord, the Lord Himself, is my strength and my
defense;

He has become my salvation."

Psalm 27:1; Isaiah 12:2

There is No Other Name

"Salvation is found in no one else,
For there is no other name under heaven given to
mankind

By which we must be saved."

"Jesus answered, 'I am the way and the truth and the life.
No one comes to the Father except through me.'"

Acts 4:12; John 14:6

Eternal Life through Jesus Christ

"For the wages of sin is death,
But the gift of God is eternal life in Christ Jesus our Lord."

"For God so loved the world that He gave His one and only Son,

That whoever believes in Him shall not perish but have eternal life."

Romans 6:23; John 3:16

Thoughts & Prayer

FAITH

Faith that Moves Mountains

"Truly I tell you if you have faith as small as a mustard seed, you can say to this mountain,
'Move from here to there,' and it will move.
Nothing will be impossible for you."

"For we live by faith, not by sight."

Matthew 17:20; 2 Corinthians 5:7

Faith Comes from Hearing

"So then faith comes by hearing,
And hearing by the word of God."

"For it is with your heart that you believe and are justified,
And it is with your mouth that you profess your faith and are saved."

Romans 10:17; Romans 10:10

Walk by Faith

"For we walk by faith, Not by sight."

"Now faith is confidence in what we hope for
And assurance about what we do not see."

"Without faith, it is impossible to please God,
Because anyone who comes to Him must believe that He
exists and that He rewards those who earnestly seek Him."

2 Corinthians 5:7; Hebrews 11:1; Hebrews 11:6

The Righteous Live by Faith

"For in the gospel, the righteousness of God is revealed—
A righteousness that is by faith from first to last,
Just as it is written: 'The righteous will live by faith.'"

"For by grace you have been saved through faith,
And that not of yourselves; it is the gift of God."

Romans 1:17; Ephesians 2:8

Shield of Faith

"In addition to all this, Take up the shield of faith,
With which you can extinguish all the flaming arrows of
the evil one."

"Fight the good fight of the faith; Take hold of the eternal
life to which you were called."

Ephesians 6:16; 1 Timothy 6:12

Thoughts & Prayer

GRACE

Saved by Grace

"For it is by grace you have been saved, through faith—
And this is not from yourselves, it is the gift of God—
Not by works, so that no one can boast."

"Where sin increased, grace increased all the more."

Ephesians 2:8-9; Romans 5:20

His Grace is Sufficient

"But He said to me, 'My grace is sufficient for you,
For my power is made perfect in weakness.'"

"For from His fullness we have all received,
Grace upon grace."

2 Corinthians 12:9; John 1:16

The Throne of Grace

"Let us then approach God's throne of grace with
confidence,

So that we may receive mercy and find grace
To help us in our time of need."

"He gives us more grace. That is why Scripture says:
'God opposes the proud but shows favor to the humble.'"

Hebrews 4:16; James 4:6

Abounding Grace

"And God is able to bless you abundantly,
So that in all things at all times, having all that you need,
You will abound in every good work."

"The grace of our Lord was poured out on me abundantly,
Along with the faith and love that are in Christ Jesus."

2 Corinthians 9:8; 1 Timothy 1:14

Grace Through Jesus Christ

"For the law was given through Moses;
Grace and truth came through Jesus Christ."

"But grow in the grace and knowledge of our Lord and
Savior Jesus Christ.
To Him be glory both now and forever!"

John 1:17; 2 Peter 3:18

Thoughts & Prayer

COVENANT

God's Covenant with Noah

"I establish my covenant with you:
Never again will all life be destroyed by the waters of a
flood;

Never again will there be a flood to destroy the earth."

"I have set my rainbow in the clouds,
And it will be the sign of the covenant between me and
the earth."

Genesis 9:11-13

Covenant with Abraham

"I will make you into a great nation,
And I will bless you;
I will make your name great, and you will be a blessing."

"And through your offspring
All nations on earth will be blessed,
Because you have obeyed me."

Genesis 12:2; Genesis 22:18

The New Covenant

"This is my blood of the covenant,
Which is poured out for many for the forgiveness of sins."

"For this is the covenant that I will make with the house of Israel after those days, declares the Lord: I will put my laws into their minds, and write them on their hearts."

Matthew 26:28; Hebrews 8:10

God's Covenant with David

"I have made a covenant with my chosen one,
I have sworn to David my servant,

'I will establish your line forever
And make your throne firm through all generations.'"

"My faithful love will be with him,
And through my name, his horn will be exalted."

Psalm 89:3-4, Psalm 89:24

The Everlasting Covenant

"I will make an everlasting covenant with you,
My faithful love promised to David."

"I will establish my covenant between me and you
And your descendants after you for the generations to
come,
To be your God and the God of your descendants after
you."

Isaiah 55:3; Genesis 17:7

Thoughts & Prayer

THE LAW AND
COMMANDMENTS

The Greatest Commandment

"'Love the Lord your God with all your heart
And with all your soul and with all your mind.'
This is the first and greatest commandment.

And the second is like it: 'Love your neighbor as yourself.'

All the Law and the Prophets hang on these two
commandments."

Matthew 22:37-40

The Law is a Guide

"Your word is a lamp for my feet,
A light on my path."

"The law of the Lord is perfect,
Refreshing the soul.

The statutes of the Lord are trustworthy,
Making wise the simple."

Psalm 119:105; Psalm 19:7

Written on Our Hearts

"This is the covenant I will make with the people of Israel
After that time, declares the Lord.

I will put my law in their minds and write it on their
hearts."

"Blessed are those who keep His statutes
And seek Him with all their heart."

Jeremiah 31:33; Psalm 119:2

The Law Fulfilled in Love

"Let no debt remain outstanding,
Except the continuing debt to love one another,

For whoever loves others has fulfilled the law.

Love does no harm to a neighbor.
Therefore love is the fulfillment of the law."

Romans 13:8, 10

Keeping His Commandments

"If you love me, keep my commands."

"Blessed rather are those who hear the word of God and obey it."

"Whoever has my commands and keeps them is the one who loves me."

John 14:15; Luke 11:28; John 14:21

Thoughts & Prayer

PROPHECY

The Spirit of Prophecy

"For prophecy never had its origin in the human will,
But prophets, though human, spoke from God
As they were carried along by the Holy Spirit."

"The testimony of Jesus is the spirit of prophecy."

2 Peter 1:21; Revelation 19:10

The Promise of the Messiah

"Therefore the Lord Himself will give you a sign:
The virgin will conceive and give birth to a son,
And will call Him Immanuel."

"For to us a child is born, to us a son is given,
And the government will be on His shoulders."

Isaiah 7:14; Isaiah 9:6

A Prophet Like Moses

"The Lord your God will raise up for you a prophet like me
from among you,
From your fellow Israelites. You must listen to Him."

"For Moses said, 'The Lord your God will raise up for you
A prophet like me from among your own people.'"

Deuteronomy 18:15; Acts 3:22

Prophecies Fulfilled in Christ

Do not think that I have come to abolish the Law or the
Prophets;
I have not come to abolish them but to fulfill them."

"For everything that was written in the past
Was written to teach us,
So that through the endurance taught in the Scriptures
and the encouragement they provide,
We might have hope."

Matthew 5:17; Romans 15:4

The Day of the Lord

"The sun will be turned to darkness and the moon to blood
Before the coming of the great and dreadful day of the
Lord."

"For the Lord Himself will come down from heaven, with a
loud command,
With the voice of the archangel and with the trumpet call
of God,
And the dead in Christ will rise first."

Joel 2:31; 1 Thessalonians 4:16

Thoughts & Prayer

THE KINGDOM OF GOD

Seek First the Kingdom

"But seek first His kingdom and His righteousness,
And all these things will be given to you as well."

"For the kingdom of God is not a matter of eating and
drinking,

But of righteousness, peace, and joy in the Holy Spirit."

Matthew 6:33; Romans 14:17

The Kingdom of Heaven is Near

"From that time on Jesus began to preach,
'Repent, for the kingdom of heaven has come near.'"

"The time has come," He said. "The kingdom of God has
come near.

Repent and believe the good news!"

Matthew 4:17; Mark 1:15

The Mustard Seed

"The kingdom of heaven is like a mustard seed,
Which a man took and planted in his field.
Though it is the smallest of all seeds,
Yet when it grows, it is the largest of garden plants
And becomes a tree, so that the birds come and perch in
its branches."

Matthew 13:31-32

Entering the Kingdom

"Truly I tell you,
Anyone who will not receive the kingdom of God like a
little child
Will never enter it."

"Very truly I tell you,
No one can see the kingdom of God unless they are born
again."

Mark 10:15; John 3:3

The Kingdom Prepared

"'Then the King will say to those on His right,
'Come, you who are blessed by my Father; take your inheritance,
The kingdom prepared for you since the creation of the world.'"

"For He has rescued us from the dominion of darkness
And brought us into the kingdom of the Son He loves."

Matthew 25:34; Colossians 1:13

Thoughts & Prayer

THE CHURCH

The Body of Christ

"Now you are the body of Christ,
And each one of you is a part of it."

"For just as each of us has one body with many members,
These members do not all have the same function."

1 Corinthians 12:27; Romans 12:4

Built on the Rock

"And I tell you that you are Peter,
And on this rock I will build my church,
And the gates of Hades will not overcome it."

"In Him the whole building is joined together
And rises to become a holy temple in the Lord."

Matthew 16:18; Ephesians 2:21

Christ is the Head of the Church

"And He is the head of the body, the church;
He is the beginning and the firstborn from among the
dead,

So that in everything He might have the supremacy."

"Christ loved the church and gave Himself up for her."

Colossians 1:18; Ephesians 5:25

The Church is the Bride of Christ

"Let us rejoice and be glad and give Him glory!
For the wedding of the Lamb has come,
And His Bride has made herself ready."

"For the marriage of the Lamb has come,
And His Bride has made herself ready."

Revelation 19:7; Revelation 19:7

One Spirit, One Body

"There is one body and one Spirit,
Just as you were called to one hope when you were called;
One Lord, one faith, one baptism."

"Now to each one the manifestation of the Spirit
Is given for the common good."

Ephesians 4:4–5; 1 Corinthians 12:7

Thoughts & Prayer

FORMING CHRIST-LIKE CHARATER

the inward life of prayer, virtue & resilience

PRAYER

Ask, Seek, Knock

"Ask and it will be given to you;
Seek and you will find;
Knock and the door will be opened to you."

"For everyone who asks receives;
The one who seeks finds;
And to the one who knocks, the door will be opened."

Matthew 7:7-8

The Lord's Prayer

"Our Father in heaven,
Hallowed be your name,
Your kingdom come, your will be done,
On earth as it is in heaven.
Give us today our daily bread."

"And forgive us our debts, as we also have forgiven our debtors."

Matthew 6:9-12

Pray Without Ceasing

"Rejoice always,
Pray without ceasing,
Give thanks in all circumstances;
For this is the will of God in Christ Jesus for you."

"Devote yourselves to prayer, being watchful and thankful."

1 Thessalonians 5:16-18; Colossians 4:2

The Power of Prayer

"The prayer of a righteous person is powerful and effective."

"If my people, who are called by my name, will humble themselves and pray
And seek my face and turn from their wicked ways,
Then I will hear from heaven, and I will forgive their sin and will heal their land."

James 5:16; 2 Chronicles 7:14

Pray in Faith

"Therefore I tell you, whatever you ask for in prayer,
Believe that you have received it, and it will be yours."

"And if we know that He hears us—whatever we ask—
We know that we have what we asked of Him."

Mark 11:24; 1 John 5:15*

Thoughts & Prayer

WORSHIP

Worship in Spirit and Truth

"God is spirit, and His worshipers must worship
In the Spirit and in truth."

"Let everything that has breath praise the Lord.
Praise the Lord."

John 4:24; Psalm 150:6

Come, Let Us Worship

"Come, let us bow down in worship,
Let us kneel before the Lord our Maker;
For He is our God
And we are the people of His pasture,
The flock under His care."

Psalm 95:6-7

The Sacrifice of Praise

"Through Jesus, therefore, let us continually offer to God
A sacrifice of praise—the fruit of lips that openly profess
His name."

"Give thanks to the Lord, for He is good;
His love endures forever."

Hebrews 13:15; 1 Chronicles 16:34

Holy, Holy, Holy

"They never stop saying:
'Holy, holy, holy is the Lord God Almighty,
Who was, and is, and is to come.'"

"Exalt the Lord our God
And worship at His footstool; He is holy."

Revelation 4:8; Psalm 99:5

Worship the Lord in the Beauty of Holiness

"Worship the Lord in the splendor of His holiness;
Tremble before Him, all the earth."

"Ascribe to the Lord the glory due His name;
Worship the Lord in the splendor of His holiness."

Psalm 96:9; Psalm 29:2

Thoughts & Prayer

LOVE

Love is Patient

"Love is patient, love is kind.
It does not envy, it does not boast, it is not proud.
It does not dishonor others, it is not self-seeking,
It is not easily angered, it keeps no record of wrongs."

"Love never fails."

1 Corinthians 13:4-5, 13:8

God's Love for Us

"For God so loved the world
That He gave His one and only Son,
That whoever believes in Him shall not perish but have
eternal life."

"But God demonstrates His own love for us in this:
While we were still sinners, Christ died for us."

John 3:16; Romans 5:8

Love One Another

"A new command I give you: Love one another.
As I have loved you, so you must love one another.
By this, everyone will know that you are my disciples,
If you love one another."

John 13:34–35

Perfect Love Casts Out Fear

"There is no fear in love.
But perfect love drives out fear,
Because fear has to do with punishment.
The one who fears is not made perfect in love."

"We love because He first loved us."

1 John 4:18–19

Love Covers a Multitude of Sins

"Above all, love each other deeply,
Because love covers over a multitude of sins."

"Let all that you do be done in love."

1 Peter 4:8; 1 Corinthians 16:14

Thoughts & Prayer

RIGHTEOUSNESS

The Lord is Our Righteousness

"This is the name by which He will be called:
The Lord Our Righteousness."

"For the Lord is righteous,
He loves justice;
The upright will see His face."

Jeremiah 23:6; Psalm 11:7

Clothed in Righteousness

"I delight greatly in the Lord;
My soul rejoices in my God.
For He has clothed me with garments of salvation
And arrayed me in a robe of His righteousness."

"He leads me in paths of righteousness for His name's
sake."

Isaiah 61:10; Psalm 23:3

Seek Righteousness

"Blessed are those who hunger and thirst for
righteousness,
For they will be filled."

"But seek first His kingdom and His righteousness,
And all these things will be given to you as well."

Matthew 5:6; Matthew 6:33

Righteousness Through Faith

"This righteousness is given through faith in Jesus Christ
To all who believe."

"He made Him who knew no sin to be sin for us,
So that in Him we might become the righteousness of
God."

Romans 3:22; 2 Corinthians 5:21

The Righteous Will Live by Faith

"For in the gospel the righteousness of God is revealed
A righteousness that is by faith from first to last,
Just as it is written: 'The righteous will live by faith.'"

"Surely the righteous will never be shaken;
They will be remembered forever."

Romans 1:17; Psalm 112:6

Thoughts & Prayer

FORGIVENESS

Forgive as the Lord Forgives

"Bear with each other and forgive one another
If any of you has a grievance against someone.
Forgive as the Lord forgave you."

"For if you forgive other people when they sin against you,
Your heavenly Father will also forgive you."

Colossians 3:13; Matthew 6:14

God's Mercy Endures Forever

"As far as the east is from the west,
So far has He removed our transgressions from us."

"The Lord our God is merciful and forgiving,
Even though we have rebelled against Him."

Psalm 103:12; Daniel 9:9

Confess and Be Forgiven

"If we confess our sins, He is faithful and just
And will forgive us our sins
And purify us from all unrighteousness."

"Come now, let us settle the matter, says the Lord.
Though your sins are like scarlet,
They shall be as white as snow."

1 John 1:9; Isaiah 1:18

Seventy Times Seven

"Then Peter came to Jesus and asked,
'Lord, how many times shall I forgive my brother or sister
who sins against me?
Up to seven times?'
Jesus answered, 'I tell you, not seven times, but seventy-
seven times.'"

"Be kind and compassionate to one another,
Forgiving each other, just as in Christ God forgave you."

Matthew 18:21-22; Ephesians 4:32

Forgiveness Through His Blood

"In Him we have redemption through His blood,
The forgiveness of sins,
In accordance with the riches of God's grace."

"Blessed is the one whose transgressions are forgiven,
Whose sins are covered."

Ephesians 1:7; Psalm 32:1

Thoughts & Prayer

HOLINESS

Be Holy, for God is Holy

"Just as He who called you is holy,
So be holy in all you do;
For it is written: 'Be holy, because I am holy.'"

"For God did not call us to be impure, but to live a holy life."

1 Peter 1:15-16; 1 Thessalonians 4:7

Perfecting Holiness

"Let us purify ourselves from everything that
contaminates body and spirit,
Perfecting holiness out of reverence for God."

"Make every effort to live in peace with everyone and to be
holy;
Without holiness no one will see the Lord."

2 Corinthians 7:1; Hebrews 12:14

Holy and Blameless

"For He chose us in Him before the creation of the world
To be holy and blameless in His sight."

"To present her to Himself as a radiant church,
Without stain or wrinkle or any other blemish,
But holy and blameless."

Ephesians 1:4; Ephesians 5:27

Offer Your Bodies as Holy Sacrifices

"Therefore, I urge you, brothers and sisters, in view of
God's mercy,
To offer your bodies as a living sacrifice, holy and pleasing
to God—
This is your true and proper worship."

"For God's temple is sacred, and you together are that
temple."

Romans 12:1; 1 Corinthians 3:17

Walk in Holiness

"Therefore, since we have these promises, dear friends,
Let us purify ourselves from everything that contaminates
body and spirit,
Perfecting holiness out of reverence for God."

"For it is God's will that you should be sanctified."

2 Corinthians 7:1; 1 Thessalonians 4:3

Thoughts & Prayer

Truth

The Word is Truth

"Sanctify them by the truth;
Your word is truth."

"For the word of the Lord is right and true;
He is faithful in all He does."

John 17:17; Psalm 33:4

Speak the Truth in Love

"Instead, speaking the truth in love,
We will grow to become in every respect the mature body
of Him who is the head, that is, Christ."

"Therefore each of you must put off falsehood and speak
truthfully to your neighbor,
For we are all members of one body."

Ephesians 4:15; Ephesians 4:25

God is the God of Truth

"He is the Rock, His works are perfect,
And all His ways are just.
A faithful God who does no wrong,
Upright and just is He."

"Guide me in Your truth and teach me,
For You are God my Savior, and my hope is in You all day
long."

Deuteronomy 32:4; Psalm 25:5

Truth Brings Freedom

"Then you will know the truth,
And the truth will set you free."

"For the fruit of the light consists in all goodness,
righteousness, and truth."

John 8:32; Ephesians 5:9

Rejoicing in the Truth

"Love does not delight in evil but rejoices with the truth."

"Whoever lives by the truth comes into the light,
So that it may be seen plainly that what they have done
has been done in the sight of God."

1 Corinthians 13:6; John 3:21

Thoughts & Prayer

WISDOM

The Fear of the Lord

"The fear of the Lord is the beginning of wisdom,
And knowledge of the Holy One is understanding."

"If any of you lacks wisdom, you should ask God,
Who gives generously to all without finding fault,
And it will be given to you."

Proverbs 9:10; James 1:5

Wisdom is Better than Gold

"How much better to get wisdom than gold,
To get insight rather than silver!"

"Blessed are those who find wisdom,
Those who gain understanding,
For she is more profitable than silver
And yields better returns than gold."

Proverbs 16:16; Proverbs 3:13–14

The Lord Gives Wisdom

"For the Lord gives wisdom;
From His mouth come knowledge and understanding."

"Whoever is wise, let him heed these things
And consider the great love of the Lord."

Proverbs 2:6; Psalm 107:43

Wisdom from Above

"But the wisdom that comes from heaven is first of all
pure;
Then peace-loving, considerate, submissive,
Full of mercy and good fruit, impartial and sincere."

"For wisdom will enter your heart,
And knowledge will be pleasant to your soul."

James 3:17; Proverbs 2:10

Walk in Wisdom

"Be very careful, then, how you live—
Not as unwise but as wise, making the most of every
opportunity."

"Walk with the wise and become wise,
For a companion of fools suffers harm."

Ephesians 5:15-16; Proverbs 13:20

Thoughts & Prayer

HOPE

Hope in the Lord

"Those who hope in the Lord will renew their strength.

They will soar on wings like eagles;
They will run and not grow weary,
They will walk and not be faint."

"For You are my hope, O Lord God."

Isaiah 40:31; Psalm 71:5

Hope Does Not Disappoint

"And hope does not put us to shame,
Because God's love has been poured out into our hearts
Through the Holy Spirit, who has been given to us."

"For in this hope we were saved."

Romans 5:5; Romans 8:24

A Living Hope

"Praise be to the God and Father of our Lord Jesus Christ!
In His great mercy He has given us new birth into a living
hope

Through the resurrection of Jesus Christ from the dead."

"We have this hope as an anchor for the soul, firm and
secure."

1 Peter 1:3; Hebrews 6:19

Hope for the Future

"'For I know the plans I have for you,' declares the Lord,
'Plans to prosper you and not to harm you,
Plans to give you hope and a future.'"

"May the God of hope fill you with all joy and peace as you
trust in Him,
So that you may overflow with hope by the power of the
Holy Spirit."

Jeremiah 29:11; Romans 15:13

Rejoice in Hope

"Rejoice in hope, be patient in tribulation,
Be constant in prayer."

"Be strong and take heart,
All you who hope in the Lord."

Romans 12:12; Psalm 31:24

Thoughts & Prayer

JOY

The Joy of the Lord

"The joy of the Lord is your strength."

"Though you have not seen Him, you love Him;
And even though you do not see Him now, you believe in Him
And are filled with an inexpressible and glorious joy."

Nehemiah 8:10; 1 Peter 1:8

Rejoice Always

"Rejoice in the Lord always.
I will say it again: Rejoice!"

"Be joyful in hope, patient in affliction, faithful in prayer."

Philippians 4:4; Romans 12:12

Joy Comes in the Morning

"Weeping may stay for the night,
But rejoicing comes in the morning."

"Those who sow with tears
Will reap with songs of joy."

Psalm 30:5; Psalm 126:5

Fullness of Joy in God's Presence

"You make known to me the path of life;
You will fill me with joy in Your presence,
With eternal pleasures at Your right hand."

"The Lord has done great things for us,
And we are filled with joy."

Psalm 16:11; Psalm 126:3

Rejoice with Gladness

"Shout for joy to the Lord, all the earth.
Worship the Lord with gladness;
Come before Him with joyful songs."

"Let the righteous rejoice in the Lord
And take refuge in Him; let all the upright in heart praise
Him!"

Psalm 100:1–2; Psalm 64:10

Thoughts & Prayer

PEACE

The Peace of God

"And the peace of God, which transcends all
understanding,
Will guard your hearts and your minds in Christ Jesus."

"Peace I leave with you; my peace I give you.
I do not give to you as the world gives.
Do not let your hearts be troubled and do not be afraid."

Philippians 4:7; John 14:27

Blessed are the Peacemakers

"Blessed are the peacemakers,
For they will be called children of God."

"Make every effort to live in peace with everyone
And to be holy; without holiness no one will see the Lord."

Matthew 5:9; Hebrews 12:14

Perfect Peace

"You will keep in perfect peace
Those whose minds are steadfast,
Because they trust in you."

"The Lord gives strength to His people;
The Lord blesses His people with peace."

Isaiah 26:3; Psalm 29:11

Peace from God

"Now may the Lord of peace Himself give you peace
At all times and in every way."

"The fruit of righteousness will be peace;
Its effect will be quietness and confidence forever."

2 Thessalonians 3:16; Isaiah 32:17

Be at Peace with Others

"If it is possible, as far as it depends on you,
Live at peace with everyone."

"Let the peace of Christ rule in your hearts,
Since as members of one body you were called to peace."

Romans 12:18; Colossians 3:15

Thoughts & Prayer

PATIENCE

The Fruit of Patience

"But the fruit of the Spirit is love, joy, peace,
Forbearance, kindness, goodness, faithfulness."

"Be completely humble and gentle;
Be patient, bearing with one another in love."

Galatians 5:22; Ephesians 4:2

Wait for the Lord

"Wait for the Lord; be strong and take heart
And wait for the Lord."

"The Lord is good to those whose hope is in Him,
To the one who seeks Him."

Psalm 27:14; Lamentations 3:25

Patience in Trials

"Let perseverance finish its work
So that you may be mature and complete, not lacking
anything."

"Be joyful in hope, patient in affliction,
Faithful in prayer."

James 1:4; Romans 12:12

God is Patient with Us

"The Lord is not slow in keeping His promise,
As some understand slowness.
Instead, He is patient with you,
Not wanting anyone to perish,
But everyone to come to repentance."

2 Peter 3:9

Clothed with Patience

"Therefore, as God's chosen people, holy and dearly loved,
Clothe yourselves with compassion, kindness, humility,
Gentleness and patience."

"Better a patient person than a warrior,
One with self-control than one who takes a city."

Colossians 3:12; Proverbs 16:32

Thoughts & Prayer

KINDNESS

Clothe Yourself with Kindness

"Therefore, as God's chosen people, holy and dearly loved,
Clothe yourselves with compassion, kindness, humility,
gentleness and patience."

"Be kind and compassionate to one another,
Forgiving each other, just as in Christ God forgave you."

Colossians 3:12; Ephesians 4:32

God's Loving Kindness

"Because your loving kindness is better than life,
My lips will glorify you."

"The Lord is righteous in all His ways
And kind in all His works."

Psalm 63:3; Psalm 145:17

Kindness Leads to Repentance

"Or do you show contempt for the riches of His kindness,
Forbearance and patience, not realizing that God's kindness
Is intended to lead you to repentance?"

"For great is His love toward us,
And the faithfulness of the Lord endures forever."

Romans 2:4; Psalm 117:2

A Heart of Kindness

"She opens her mouth with wisdom,
And the teaching of kindness is on her tongue."

"Love is patient, love is kind.
It does not envy, it does not boast, it is not proud."

Proverbs 31:26; 1 Corinthians 13:4

Kindness in Action

"Let love and faithfulness never leave you;
Bind them around your neck, write them on the tablet of
your heart."

"Do not let any unwholesome talk come out of your
mouths,
But only what is helpful for building others up according
to their needs,
That it may benefit those who listen."

Proverbs 3:3; Ephesians 4:29

Thoughts & Prayer

SELF-CONTROL

The Fruit of Self-Control

"But the fruit of the Spirit is love, joy, peace,
Forbearance, kindness, goodness, faithfulness,
Gentleness and self-control.
Against such things there is no law."

Galatians 5:22-23

A City Without Walls

"Like a city whose walls are broken through
Is a person who lacks self-control."

"For the grace of God has appeared that offers salvation to
all people.
It teaches us to say 'No' to ungodliness and worldly
passions,
And to live self-controlled, upright, and godly lives in this
present age."

Proverbs 25:28; Titus 2:11-12

Control Your Tongue

"Those who guard their mouths and their tongues
Keep themselves from calamity."

"Everyone should be quick to listen, slow to speak
And slow to become angry, because human anger
Does not produce the righteousness that God desires."

Proverbs 21:23; James 1:19-20

Discipline and Self-Control

"No discipline seems pleasant at the time, but painful.
Later on, however, it produces a harvest of righteousness
and peace
For those who have been trained by it."

"Better a patient person than a warrior,
One with self-control than one who takes a city."

Hebrews 12:11; Proverbs 16:32

Self-Control and Eternal Life

"To those who by persistence in doing good seek glory,
honor and immortality,
He will give eternal life."

"For this very reason, make every effort to add to your faith goodness;
And to goodness, knowledge; and to knowledge, self-control;
And to self-control, perseverance."

Romans 2:7; 2 Peter 1:5-6

Thoughts & Prayer

FAITHFULNESS

God's Faithfulness is Forever

"For the Lord is good and His love endures forever;
His faithfulness continues through all generations."

"Your faithfulness endures to all generations;
You have established the earth, and it stands fast."

Psalm 100:5; Psalm 119:90

Faithful in Small Things

"Whoever can be trusted with very little
Can also be trusted with much."

"His master replied, 'Well done, good and faithful servant!
You have been faithful with a few things;
I will put you in charge of many things. Come and share
your master's happiness!'"

Luke 16:10; Matthew 25:23

Great is Your Faithfulness

"Because of the Lord's great love we are not consumed,
For His compassions never fail.
They are new every morning; great is Your faithfulness."

"The Lord is faithful, and He will strengthen you
And protect you from the evil one."

Lamentations 3:22-23; 2 Thessalonians 3:3

Walking in Faithfulness

"Let love and faithfulness never leave you;
Bind them around your neck,
Write them on the tablet of your heart."

"Be faithful, even to the point of death,
And I will give you life as your victor's crown."

Proverbs 3:3; Revelation 2:10

Faithful in Prayer

"Be joyful in hope, patient in affliction,
Faithful in prayer."

"The one who calls you is faithful,
And He will do it."

Romans 12:12; 1 Thessalonians 5:24

Thoughts & Prayer

MERCY

The Lord is Full of Mercy

"The Lord is compassionate and gracious,
Slow to anger, abounding in love."

"For as high as the heavens are above the earth,
So great is His love for those who fear Him."

Psalm 103:8; Psalm 103:11

His Mercies Are New Every Morning

"Because of the Lord's great love we are not consumed,
For His compassions never fail.
They are new every morning; great is Your faithfulness."

"Remember, Lord, Your great mercy and love,
For they are from of old."

Lamentations 3:22-23; Psalm 25:6

Blessed are the Merciful

"Blessed are the merciful,
For they will be shown mercy."

"He has shown you, O mortal, what is good.
And what does the Lord require of you?
To act justly and to love mercy
And to walk humbly with your God."

Matthew 5:7; Micah 6:8

God's Mercy Endures Forever

"Give thanks to the Lord, for He is good;
His mercy endures forever."

"Let the wicked forsake their ways
And the unrighteous their thoughts.
Let them turn to the Lord, and He will have mercy on
them."

Psalm 136:1; Isaiah 55:7

Mercy Leads to Forgiveness

"For I will forgive their wickedness
And will remember their sins no more."

"Let us then approach God's throne of grace with
confidence,
So that we may receive mercy and find grace to help us in
our time of need."

Hebrews 8:12; Hebrews 4:16

Thoughts & Prayer

LAW

The Law of the Lord is Perfect

"The law of the Lord is perfect,
Refreshing the soul.
The statutes of the Lord are trustworthy,
Making wise the simple."

"The precepts of the Lord are right,
Giving joy to the heart."

Psalm 19:7–8

Meditate on His Law

"Blessed is the one who does not walk in step with the
wicked,

But whose delight is in the law of the Lord,
And who meditates on His law day and night."

"They are like a tree planted by streams of water,
Which yields its fruit in season."

Psalm 1:1–3

The Law of Love

"Love does no harm to a neighbor.
Therefore love is the fulfillment of the law."

"Whoever loves others has fulfilled the law."

Romans 13:10, Romans 13:8

The Law and the Prophets

"So in everything, do to others what you would have them do to you,
For this sums up the Law and the Prophets."

"Teacher, which is the greatest commandment in the Law?

Jesus replied: 'Love the Lord your God with all your heart
And with all your soul and with all your mind.'
This is the first and greatest commandment."

Matthew 7:12; Matthew 22:36-38

Written on Our Hearts

"This is the covenant I will make with the people of Israel after that time, declares the Lord.
I will put my law in their minds and write it on their hearts."

"I will be their God, and they will be my people."

Jeremiah 31:33

Thoughts & Prayer

JUSTICE

The Lord Loves Justice

"For the Lord is righteous,
He loves justice;
The upright will see His face."

"For I, the Lord, love justice;
I hate robbery and wrongdoing."

Psalm 11:7; Isaiah 61:8

Act Justly

"He has shown you, O mortal, what is good.
And what does the Lord require of you?
To act justly and to love mercy
And to walk humbly with your God."

"Follow justice and justice alone,
So that you may live and possess the land the Lord your
God is giving you."

Micah 6:8; Deuteronomy 16:20

Justice for the Oppressed

"The Lord works righteousness
And justice for all the oppressed."

"Learn to do right; seek justice.
Defend the oppressed.
Take up the cause of the fatherless;
Plead the case of the widow."

Psalm 103:6; Isaiah 1:17

Let Justice Roll On

"But let justice roll on like a river,
Righteousness like a never-failing stream!"

"Speak up for those who cannot speak for themselves,
For the rights of all who are destitute."

Amos 5:24; Proverbs 31:8

Justice is God's Delight

"To do what is right and just
Is more acceptable to the Lord than sacrifice."

"Righteousness and justice are the foundation of your throne;
Love and faithfulness go before you."

Proverbs 21:3; Psalm 89:14

Thoughts & Prayer

HUMILITY

Humble Yourselves Before the Lord

"Humble yourselves before the Lord,
And He will lift you up."

"For all those who exalt themselves will be humbled,
And those who humble themselves will be exalted."

James 4:10; Luke 14:11

Clothe Yourselves with Humility

"All of you, clothe yourselves with humility toward one
another,
Because, 'God opposes the proud but shows favor to the
humble.'"

"Humble yourselves, therefore, under God's mighty hand,
That He may lift you up in due time."

1 Peter 5:5–6

Walk Humbly with God

"He has shown you, O mortal, what is good.
And what does the Lord require of you?
To act justly and to love mercy
And to walk humbly with your God."

Micah 6:8

A Humble Heart

"The Lord is close to the brokenhearted
And saves those who are crushed in spirit."

"For this is what the high and exalted One says—
He who lives forever, whose name is holy:
'I live in a high and holy place,
But also with the one who is contrite and lowly in spirit.'"

Psalm 34:18; Isaiah 57:15

God Gives Grace to the Humble

"Whoever humbles themselves like this child
Is the greatest in the kingdom of heaven."

"But He gives us more grace. That is why Scripture says:
'God opposes the proud but shows favor to the humble.'"

Matthew 18:4; James 4:6

Thoughts & Prayer

OBEDIENCE

Blessed Through Obedience

"Blessed are all who fear the Lord,
Who walk in obedience to Him."

"Now that you know these things,
You will be blessed if you do them."

Psalm 128:1; John 13:17

Obedience is Better than Sacrifice

"To obey is better than sacrifice,
And to heed is better than the fat of rams."

"If you love me, keep my commands."

1 Samuel 15:22; John 14:15

Obey God's Voice

"Whether you turn to the right or to the left,
Your ears will hear a voice behind you, saying,
'This is the way; walk in it.'"

"Blessed are those who hear the word of God and obey it."

Isaiah 30:21; Luke 11:28

Walk in Obedience to God

"Walk in obedience to all that the Lord your God has
commanded you,
So that you may live and prosper and prolong your days."

"Anyone who loves me will obey my teaching.
My Father will love them, and we will come to them and
make our home with them."

Deuteronomy 5:33; John 14:23

Obedience Brings Joy

"If you keep my commands, you will remain in my love,
Just as I have kept my Father's commands and remain in
His love.

I have told you this so that my joy may be in you
And that your joy may be complete."

John 15:10-11

Thoughts & Prayer

KINGDOM LIVING & MISSION

walking it out in the community and the wider world

LEADERSHIP AND AUTHORITY

Servant Leadership

"Whoever wants to become great among you must be your servant,

And whoever wants to be first must be your slave—
Just as the Son of Man did not come to be served, but to serve,
And to give His life as a ransom for many."

Matthew 20:26-28

Appointed by God

"Let everyone be subject to the governing authorities,
For there is no authority except that which God has established."

"For rulers hold no terror for those who do right,
But for those who do wrong."

Romans 13:1, 3

Shepherd the Flock

"Be shepherds of God's flock that is under your care,
Watching over them—not because you must, but because
you are willing,
As God wants you to be;
Not pursuing dishonest gain, but eager to serve."

1 Peter 5:2

Wisdom for Leaders

"If any of you lacks wisdom,
You should ask God, who gives generously to all without
finding fault,
And it will be given to you."

"Where there is no guidance, a people falls,
But in an abundance of counselors there is safety."

James 1:5; Proverbs 11:14

Lead with Diligence

"If your gift is leadership, do it diligently."

"Do nothing out of selfish ambition or vain conceit. Rather, in humility value others above yourselves."

Romans 12:8; Philippians 2:3

Thoughts & Prayer

SPIRITUAL GIFTS

Gifts from the Spirit

"There are different kinds of gifts, but the same Spirit distributes them."

"To each one the manifestation of the Spirit is given for the common good."

"Now to each one the manifestation of the Spirit is given for the common good."

1 Corinthians 12:4; 1 Corinthians 12:7

One Body, Many Gifts

"Just as each of us has one body with many members,
And these members do not all have the same function,
So in Christ we, though many, form one body,
And each member belongs to all the others."

Romans 12:4–5

Gifts of Prophecy and Service

"If your gift is prophesying, then prophesy in accordance
with your faith;
If it is serving, then serve; if it is teaching, then teach."

"We have different gifts, according to the grace given to
each of us."

Romans 12:6–7

Use Your Gifts in Love

"If I speak in the tongues of men or of angels, but do not
have love,
I am only a resounding gong or a clanging cymbal."

"The greatest of these is love."

1 Corinthians 13:1; 1 Corinthians 13:13

Stir Up the Gift of God

"For this reason I remind you to fan into flame the gift of
God,
Which is in you through the laying on of my hands."

"Each of you should use whatever gift you have received
to serve others,
As faithful stewards of God's grace in its various forms."

2 Timothy 1:6; 1 Peter 4:10

Thoughts & Prayer

MIRACLES

God of Wonders

"You are the God who performs miracles;
You display Your power among the peoples."

"For nothing is impossible with God."

Psalm 77:14; Luke 1:37

Jesus Heals the Sick

"Jesus went through all the towns and villages,
Teaching in their synagogues, proclaiming the good news
of the kingdom
And healing every disease and sickness."

"By His wounds we are healed."

Matthew 9:35; Isaiah 53:5

Feeding the Multitudes

Taking the five loaves and the two fish and looking up to heaven,
He gave thanks and broke the loaves.
Then He gave them to the disciples,
And the disciples gave them to the people."

"They all ate and were satisfied.".

Matthew 14:19-20

The Blind Will See

"Then will the eyes of the blind be opened
And the ears of the deaf unstopped.
Then will the lame leap like a deer,
And the mute tongue shout for joy."

"Jesus said, 'Go, your faith has healed you.'"

Isaiah 35:5-6; Mark 10:52

The Dead Are Raised

"Jesus called in a loud voice, 'Lazarus, come out!'
The dead man came out, his hands and feet wrapped with
strips of linen."

"I am the resurrection and the life.
The one who believes in Me will live, even though they
die."

John 11:43-44; John 11:25

Thoughts & Prayer

PARABLES OF JESUS

The Parable of the Sower

"A farmer went out to sow his seed.
As he was scattering the seed, some fell along the path,
And the birds came and ate it up.
Other seed fell on good soil,
Where it produced a crop—a hundred, sixty, or thirty times
what was sown."

"Whoever has ears, let them hear."

Matthew 13:3-4; Matthew 13:8-9

The Good Samaritan

"A man was going down from Jerusalem to Jericho,
When he was attacked by robbers.
A Samaritan, as he traveled, came where the man was;
And when he saw him, he took pity on him."

"Go and do likewise."

Luke 15:13, 20, 24 Luke 10:30; Luke 10:33, 37

The Parable of the Lost Sheep

"Suppose one of you has a hundred sheep and loses one of them. Doesn't he leave the ninety-nine in the open country, And go after the lost sheep until he finds it?"

"In the same way, there will be more rejoicing in heaven over one sinner who repents
Than over ninety-nine righteous persons who do not need to repent."

Luke 15:4, 7

The Prodigal Son

"The younger son got together all he had,
Set off for a distant country and there squandered his wealth in wild living.
But while he was still a long way off, his father saw him
And was filled with compassion for him;
He ran to his son, threw his arms around him and kissed him."

"For this son of mine was dead and is alive again;
He was lost and is found."

Luke 15:20-21: Luke 15:13

The Parable of the Talents

"Well done, good and faithful servant!
You have been faithful with a few things;
I will put you in charge of many things."

"To everyone who has, more will be given,
And they will have an abundance.
Whoever does not have, even what they have will be taken
from them."

Matthew 25:21, 29

Thoughts & Prayer

HEALING

By His Wounds We Are Healed

"But He was pierced for our transgressions,
He was crushed for our iniquities;
The punishment that brought us peace was on Him,
And by His wounds we are healed."

"The Lord sustains them on their sickbed
And restores them from their bed of illness."

Isaiah 53:5; Psalm 41:3

Jesus Heals the Blind

"As Jesus and His disciples were leaving Jericho,
A large crowd followed Him.
Two blind men were sitting by the roadside, and when
they heard that Jesus was going by,
They shouted, 'Lord, Son of David, have mercy on us!'"

"Jesus had compassion on them and touched their eyes.
Immediately they received their sight and followed Him."

Matthew 20:29–30, 34

The Power of Faith to Heal

"Jesus said to her, 'Daughter, your faith has healed you.
Go in peace and be freed from your suffering.'"

"Therefore confess your sins to each other and pray for
each other
So that you may be healed.
The prayer of a righteous person is powerful and
effective."

Mark 5:34; James 5:16

Heal the Sick

"Is anyone among you sick? Let them call the elders of the
church to pray over them
And anoint them with oil in the name of the Lord."

"Heal the sick, raise the dead, cleanse those who have
leprosy, drive out demons.
Freely you have received; freely give."

James 5:14; Matthew 10:8

God is the Healer

"Lord, my God, I called to you for help, and you healed me."

"He heals the brokenhearted and binds up their wounds."

"Praise the Lord, my soul, and forget not all His benefits—Who forgives all your sins and heals all your diseases."

Psalm 30:2; Psalm 147:3; Psalm 103:2–3

Thoughts & Prayer

GOD'S PROMISES

The Lord is Faithful to His Promises

"The Lord is trustworthy in all He promises
And faithful in all He does."

"For no matter how many promises God has made,
They are 'Yes' in Christ. And so through Him the 'Amen'
Is spoken by us to the glory of God."

Psalm 145:13; 2 Corinthians 1:20

Promises for Those Who Love Him

"And we know that in all things God works for the good of
those who love Him,
Who have been called according to His purpose."

"No good thing does He withhold
From those whose walk is blameless."

Romans 8:28; Psalm 84:11

A Promise of Peace

"You will keep in perfect peace
Those whose minds are steadfast, because they trust in
you."

"Peace I leave with you; my peace I give you.
I do not give to you as the world gives.
Do not let your hearts be troubled and do not be afraid."

Isaiah 26:3; John 14:27

God Will Never Leave You

"Be strong and courageous. Do not be afraid or terrified
because of them,
For the Lord your God goes with you;
He will never leave you nor forsake you."

"The Lord is my helper; I will not be afraid.
What can mere mortals do to me?"

Deuteronomy 31:6; Hebrews 13:6

Eternal Life is Promised

"And this is what He promised us—eternal life."

"For God so loved the world that He gave His one and only Son,
That whoever believes in Him shall not perish but have eternal life."

1 John 2:25; John 3:16

Thoughts & Prayer

FEAR OF THE LORD

The Beginning of Wisdom

"The fear of the Lord is the beginning of wisdom,
And knowledge of the Holy One is understanding."

"The fear of the Lord is a fountain of life,
Turning a person from the snares of death."

Proverbs 9:10; Proverbs 14:27

Fear God and Keep His Commandments

"Now all has been heard; here is the conclusion of the
matter:
Fear God and keep His commandments,
For this is the duty of all mankind."

"To fear the Lord is to hate evil;
I hate pride and arrogance,
Evil behavior and perverse speech."

Ecclesiastes 12:13; Proverbs 8:13

Blessed are Those Who Fear the Lord

"Blessed are all who fear the Lord,
Who walk in obedience to Him."

"He fulfills the desires of those who fear Him;
He hears their cry and saves them."

Psalm 128:1; Psalm 145:19

The Lord Delights in Those Who Fear Him

"The Lord delights in those who fear Him,
Who put their hope in His unfailing love."

"As a father has compassion on his children,
So the Lord has compassion on those who fear Him."

Psalm 147:11; Psalm 103:13

Fear of the Lord Leads to Life

"The fear of the Lord leads to life;
Then one rests content, untouched by trouble."

"Let all the earth fear the Lord;
Let all the people of the world revere Him."

Proverbs 19:23; Psalm 33:8

Thoughts & Prayer

UNITY

Unity in Christ

"There is one body and one Spirit,
Just as you were called to one hope when you were called;
One Lord, one faith, one baptism;
One God and Father of all,
Who is over all and through all and in all."

Ephesians 4:4-6

Dwelling Together in Unity

"How good and pleasant it is
When God's people live together in unity!"

"For where two or three gather in my name,
There am I with them."

Psalm 133:1; Matthew 18:20

Unity Through Love

"Make my joy complete by being like-minded,
Having the same love, being one in spirit and of one mind."

"Above all, love each other deeply,
Because love covers over a multitude of sins."

Philippians 2:2; 1 Peter 4:8

Striving for Unity

"Make every effort to keep the unity of the Spirit
Through the bond of peace."

"Let us therefore make every effort to do what leads to peace
And to mutual edification."

Ephesians 4:3; Romans 14:19

Perfect Unity in Love

"And over all these virtues put on love,
Which binds them all together in perfect unity."

"May the God who gives endurance and encouragement
give you the same attitude of mind
Toward each other that Christ Jesus had, so that with one
mind and one voice
You may glorify the God and Father of our Lord Jesus
Christ."

Colossians 3:14; Romans 15:5-6

Thoughts & Prayer

STEWARDSHIP AND MONEY

Treasures in Heaven

"Do not store up for yourselves treasures on earth,
Where moths and vermin destroy,
And where thieves break in and steal.
But store up for yourselves treasures in heaven."

"For where your treasure is, there your heart will be also."

Matthew 6:19-21

God Loves a Cheerful Giver

"Each of you should give what you have decided in your
heart to give,

Not reluctantly or under compulsion,
For God loves a cheerful giver."

"Freely you have received; freely give."

2 Corinthians 9:7; Matthew 10:8

The Lord's Steward

"Moreover, it is required of stewards that they be found faithful."

"Whoever can be trusted with very little
Can also be trusted with much,
And whoever is dishonest with very little will also be dishonest with much."

1 Corinthians 4:2; Luke 16:10

The Earth is the Lord's

"The earth is the Lord's, and everything in it,
The world, and all who live in it."

"Honor the Lord with your wealth,
With the firstfruits of all your crops;

Then your barns will be filled to overflowing."

Psalm 24:1; Proverbs 3:9-10

Contentment in All Things

"Keep your lives free from the love of money
And be content with what you have,
Because God has said,
'Never will I leave you; never will I forsake you.'"

"For godliness with contentment is great gain."

Hebrews 13:5; 1 Timothy 6:6

Thoughts & Prayer

GENEROSITY

God Loves a Cheerful Giver

"Each of you should give what you have decided in your
heart to give,
Not reluctantly or under compulsion,
For God loves a cheerful giver."

"Freely you have received; freely give."

2 Corinthians 9:7; Matthew 10:8

Generous Souls are Blessed

"A generous person will prosper;
Whoever refreshes others will be refreshed."

"Give, and it will be given to you.
A good measure, pressed down, shaken together and
running over,
Will be poured into your lap."

Proverbs 11:25; Luke 6:38

It is More Blessed to Give

"In everything I did, I showed you that by this kind of hard work
We must help the weak, remembering the words the Lord Jesus Himself said:
'It is more blessed to give than to receive.'"

"Good will come to those who are generous and lend freely,
Who conduct their affairs with justice."

Acts 20:35; Psalm 112:5

Give to the Needy

"Whoever is kind to the poor lends to the Lord,
And He will reward them for what they have done."

"Sell your possessions and give to the poor.
Provide purses for yourselves that will not wear out,
A treasure in heaven that will never fail."

Proverbs 19:17; Luke 12:33

The Gift of Generosity

"You will be enriched in every way
So that you can be generous on every occasion,
And through us your generosity will result in thanksgiving
to God."

"Command them to do good, to be rich in good deeds,
And to be generous and willing to share."

2 Corinthians 9:11; 1 Timothy 6:18

Thoughts & Prayer

TRIALS, STRENGTH & ETERNAL HOPE

how faith endures and triumphs

SIN

All Have Sinned

"For all have sinned
And fall short of the glory of God."

"There is no one righteous, not even one;
There is no one who understands,
No one who seeks God."

Romans 3:23; Romans 3:10-11

The Wages of Sin

"For the wages of sin is death,
But the gift of God is eternal life In Christ Jesus our Lord."

"Sin entered the world through one man, and death through sin,

And in this way, death came to all people, because all sinned."

Romans 6:23; Romans 5:12

If We Confess Our Sins

"If we confess our sins,
He is faithful and just and will forgive us our sins
And purify us from all unrighteousness."

"As far as the east is from the west,
So far has He removed our transgressions from us."

1 John 1:9; Psalm 103:12

Temptation and Sin

"No temptation has overtaken you except what is
common to mankind.

And God is faithful; He will not let you be tempted beyond
what you can bear.

But when you are tempted, He will also provide a way out
So that you can endure it."

"Resist the devil, and he will flee from you."

1 Corinthians 10:13; James 4:7

The Blood that Cleanses

"But if we walk in the light, as He is in the light,
We have fellowship with one another,
And the blood of Jesus, His Son, purifies us from all sin."

"In Him we have redemption through His blood,
The forgiveness of sins, in accordance with the riches of
God's grace."

1 John 1:7; Ephesians 1:7

Thoughts & Prayer

SUFFERING

Strength in Suffering

"But He said to me, 'My grace is sufficient for you,
For my power is made perfect in weakness.'
Therefore I will boast all the more gladly about my
weaknesses,

So that Christ's power may rest on me."

"For when I am weak, then I am strong."

2 Corinthians 12:9-10

Suffering for Righteousness

"But even if you should suffer for what is right, you are blessed.
Do not fear their threats; do not be frightened."

"If you suffer as a Christian, do not be ashamed,
But praise God that you bear that name."

1 Peter 3:14; 1 Peter 4:16

The Testing of Your Faith

"Consider it pure joy, my brothers and sisters,
Whenever you face trials of many kinds,
Because you know that the testing of your faith produces perseverance."

"For our light and momentary troubles are achieving for us an eternal glory
That far outweighs them all."

James 1:2-3; 2 Corinthians 4:17

Sharing in Christ's Suffering

"I want to know Christ—yes, to know the power of His resurrection
And participation in His sufferings,
Becoming like Him in His death."

"If we share in His sufferings, we may also share in His glory."

Philippians 3:10; Romans 8:17

The God of All Comfort

"Praise be to the God and Father of our Lord Jesus Christ,
The Father of compassion and the God of all comfort,
Who comforts us in all our troubles,
So that we can comfort those in any trouble
With the comfort we ourselves receive from God."

2 Corinthians 1:3-4

Thoughts & Prayer

REPENTANCE

Repent and Turn to God

"Repent, then, and turn to God,
So that your sins may be wiped out,
That times of refreshing may come from the Lord."

"If we confess our sins, He is faithful and just
And will forgive us our sins and purify us from all
unrighteousness."

Acts 3:19; 1 John 1:9

God's Kindness Leads to Repentance

"Or do you show contempt for the riches of His kindness,
Forbearance, and patience, not realizing that God's
kindness
Is intended to lead you to repentance?"

"The sacrifices of God are a broken spirit;
A broken and contrite heart, O God, you will not despise."

Romans 2:4; Psalm 51:17

Repent and Believe the Good News

"The time has come," He said.
"The kingdom of God has come near.
Repent and believe the good news!"

"In the past God overlooked such ignorance,
But now He commands all people everywhere to repent."

Mark 1:15; Acts 17:30

A Heart of Repentance

"Create in me a pure heart, O God,
And renew a steadfast spirit within me."

"Have mercy on me, O God,
According to your unfailing love;
According to your great compassion
Blot out my transgressions."

Psalm 51:10; Psalm 51:1

God Desires Repentance

"The Lord is not slow in keeping His promise, as some understand slowness.
Instead He is patient with you,
Not wanting anyone to perish,
But everyone to come to repentance."

"I tell you, there will be more rejoicing in heaven over one sinner who repents
Than over ninety-nine righteous persons who do not need to repent."

2 Peter 3:9; Luke 15:7

Thoughts & Prayer

COURAGE

Be Strong and Courageous

"Be strong and courageous. Do not be afraid;
Do not be discouraged, for the Lord your God will be with
you wherever you go."

"Wait for the Lord; be strong and take heart
And wait for the Lord."

Joshua 1:9; Psalm 27:14

The Lord is My Light

"The Lord is my light and my salvation—whom shall I fear?
The Lord is the stronghold of my life—of whom shall I be
afraid?"

"Though an army besiege me, my heart will not fear;
Though war break out against me, even then I will be
confident."

Psalm 27:1, 27:3

Fear Not, For I Am With You

"So do not fear, for I am with you;
Do not be dismayed, for I am your God.
I will strengthen you and help you;
I will uphold you with my righteous right hand."

"Even though I walk through the darkest valley,
I will fear no evil, for You are with me."

Isaiah 41:10; Psalm 23:4

Courage from the Lord

"Be on your guard; stand firm in the faith;
Be courageous; be strong."

"The Lord is with me; I will not be afraid.
What can mere mortals do to me?"

1 Corinthians 16:13; Psalm 118:6

Courage in the Face of Trials

"I have told you these things, so that in me you may have peace.
In this world you will have trouble.
But take heart! I have overcome the world."

"The name of the Lord is a fortified tower;
The righteous run to it and are safe."

John 16:33; Proverbs 18:10

Thoughts & Prayer

STRENGTH

The Lord is My Strength

"The Lord is my strength and my shield;
My heart trusts in Him, and He helps me."

"I can do all this through Him who gives me strength."

Psalm 28:7; Philippians 4:13

Strength in Weakness

"But He said to me, 'My grace is sufficient for you,
For my power is made perfect in weakness.'
Therefore I will boast all the more gladly about my weaknesses,
So that Christ's power may rest on me."

2 Corinthians 12:9

Strength for the Weary

"He gives strength to the weary
And increases the power of the weak."

"Even youths grow tired and weary,
And young men stumble and fall;
But those who hope in the Lord
Will renew their strength."

Isaiah 40:29-31

Be Strong in the Lord

"Finally, be strong in the Lord and in His mighty power."

"The Lord gives strength to His people;
The Lord blesses His people with peace."

Ephesians 6:10; Psalm 29:11

Strength from God's Presence

"Do not grieve, for the joy of the Lord is your strength."

"God is our refuge and strength,
An ever-present help in trouble."

Nehemiah 8:10; Psalm 46:1

Thoughts & Prayer

PERSEVERANCE

Perseverance Produces Character

"Not only so, but we also glory in our sufferings,
Because we know that suffering produces perseverance;
Perseverance, character; and character, hope."

"Let us run with perseverance the race marked out for us,
Fixing our eyes on Jesus, the pioneer and perfecter of
faith."

Romans 5:3-4; Hebrews 12:1-2

Blessed are Those Who Persevere

"Blessed is the one who perseveres under trial
Because, having stood the test, that person will receive
the crown of life
That the Lord has promised to those who love Him."

"Consider it pure joy, my brothers and sisters,
Whenever you face trials of many kinds,
Because you know that the testing of your faith produces
perseverance."

James 1:12; James 1:2-3

Do Not Grow Weary

"Let us not become weary in doing good,
For at the proper time we will reap a harvest if we do not give up."

"But the one who stands firm to the end will be saved."

Galatians 6:9; Matthew 24:13

Perseverance in Faith

"For you have need of endurance, so that when you have done the will of God
You may receive what is promised."

"Be joyful in hope, patient in affliction, faithful in prayer."

Hebrews 10:36; Romans 12:12

Keep Pressing On

"Brothers and sisters, I do not consider myself yet to have taken hold of it.
But one thing I do: Forgetting what is behind and straining toward what is ahead,
I press on toward the goal to win the prize
For which God has called me heavenward in Christ Jesus."

Philippians 3:13-14

Thoughts & Prayer

JUDGMENT

The Day of Judgment

"For we must all appear before the judgment seat of
Christ,
So that each of us may receive what is due us
For the things done while in the body, whether good or
bad."

"For God will bring every deed into judgment,
Including every hidden thing, whether it is good or evil."

2 Corinthians 5:10; Ecclesiastes 12:14

Righteous Judgment

"The Lord is a God who avenges.
O God who avenges, shine forth."

"But the Lord sits enthroned forever;
He has established His throne for judgment.
He rules the world in righteousness
And judges the peoples with equity."

Psalm 94:1; Psalm 9:7-8

Judge Not

"Do not judge, or you too will be judged.
For in the same way you judge others, you will be judged,
And with the measure you use, it will be measured to you."

"Therefore, let us stop passing judgment on one another."

Matthew 7:1-2; Romans 14:13

The Great White Throne

"Then I saw a great white throne and Him who was seated
on it.
The earth and the heavens fled from His presence,
And there was no place for them."

"Each person was judged according to what they had
done."

Revelation 20:11; Revelation 20:13

The Book of Life

"Anyone whose name was not found written in the book of life
Was thrown into the lake of fire."

"He who overcomes will, like them, be dressed in white.
I will never blot out the name of that person from the book of life."

Revelation 20:15; Revelation 3:5

Thoughts & Prayer

ETERNAL LIFE

The Gift of Eternal Life

"For the wages of sin is death,
But the gift of God is eternal life
In Christ Jesus our Lord."

"And this is the testimony: God has given us eternal life,
And this life is in His Son."

Romans 6:23; 1 John 5:11

Believe and Have Eternal Life

"For God so loved the world that He gave His one and only Son,

That whoever believes in Him shall not perish but have eternal life."

"Whoever believes in the Son has eternal life,
But whoever rejects the Son will not see life."

John 3:16; John 3:36

Eternal Life through Jesus Christ

"Now this is eternal life: that they know You,
The only true God, and Jesus Christ, whom You have sent."

"I give them eternal life, and they shall never perish;
No one will snatch them out of my hand."

John 17:3; John 10:28

The Promise of Eternal Life

"And this is what He promised us—eternal life."

"For we know that if the earthly tent we live in is
destroyed,

We have a building from God,
An eternal house in heaven, not built by human hands."

1 John 2:25; 2 Corinthians 5:1

Inheritance of Eternal Life

"To those who by persistence in doing good
Seek glory, honor, and immortality,
He will give eternal life."

"Everyone who has left houses or brothers or sisters or
father or mother or wife or children or fields for my sake
Will receive a hundred times as much and will inherit
eternal life."

Romans 2:7; Matthew 19:29

Thoughts & Prayer

GOD'S GLORY IN CREATION

CREATION

In the Beginning

"In the beginning God created the heavens and the earth."

"The earth is the Lord's, and everything in it,
The world, and all who live in it."

Genesis 1:1; Psalm 24:1

The Heavens Declare

*"The heavens declare the glory of God;
The skies proclaim the work of His hands."*

*"For since the creation of the world God's invisible
qualities—His eternal power and divine nature—
Have been clearly seen, being understood from what has
been made."*

Psalm 19:1; Romans 1:20

Fearfully and Wonderfully Made

"For You created my inmost being;
You knit me together in my mother's womb."

"I praise You because I am fearfully and wonderfully made;
Your works are wonderful, I know that full well."

Psalm 139:13-14

All Things Were Made by Him

"Through Him all things were made;
Without Him nothing was made that has been made."

"For in Him all things were created: things in heaven and
on earth,
Visible and invisible, whether thrones or powers or rulers
or authorities."

John 1:3; Colossians 1:16

God's Handiwork

"For we are God's handiwork,
Created in Christ Jesus to do good works,
Which God prepared in advance for us to do."

"By the word of the Lord the heavens were made,
Their starry host by the breath of His mouth."

Ephesians 2:10; Psalm 33:6

Thoughts & Prayer

THE FIRMAMENT

The Glory of the Firmament

"The heavens declare the glory of God;
and the firmament sheweth his handywork."

"And God said, Let there be a firmament in the midst of
the waters,
and let it divide the waters from the waters."

Psalm 19:1 Genesis 1:6

The Witness Above

"And God made the firmament,
and divided the waters which were under the firmament
from the waters which were above the firmament:
and it was so. "It is he that sitteth upon the circle of the
earth,
and the inhabitants thereof are as grasshoppers;
that stretcheth out the heavens as a curtain,
and spreadeth them out as a tent to dwell in."

Genesis 1:7 Isaiah 40:22

Proclaiming His Power

"And above the firmament that was over their heads
was the likeness of a throne,
as the appearance of a sapphire stone:
and upon the likeness of the throne was the likeness
as the appearance of a man above upon it."

"The heavens declare his righteousness,
and all the people see his glory."

Ezekiel 1:26 Psalm 97:6

A Dwelling Place

"And God called the firmament Heaven.
And the evening and the morning were the second day."

"The Lord by wisdom hath founded the earth;
by understanding hath he established the heavens."

Genesis 1:8 Proverbs 3:19

Eternal Praise

"Praise ye the Lord. Praise God in his sanctuary:
praise him in the firmament of his power."

"To him that stretched out the earth above the waters:
for his mercy endureth for ever."

Psalm 150:1 Psalm 136:6

Thoughts & Prayer

TOOLS AND CLOSING REFLECTIONS

Here's a simple step-by-step guide to creating your own Bible verse poems:

Step 1: Choose a Theme
- Think about a subject you want to express (like Love, Faith, Hope, or Forgiveness).
- Be as specific as you like! For example, under "Faith," you could focus on "Faith During Hard Times" or "Growing Faith."

Step 2: Find Related Verses
- Search for Bible verses that match your theme. You can use a Bible app, a concordance, or a search engine to find verses about your topic.
- Choose 2-4 verses that speak to different aspects of your theme or reinforce each other.

Step 3: Put the Verses in Order
- Arrange the verses in a way that flows naturally.
- Think of it like telling a story or building on an idea—each verse should add to the last.

Step 4: Avoid Adding Extra Words
- Only use the words from the Bible verses. This keeps the poem authentic and focused.
- If a verse has extra parts that don't fit your theme, feel free to use only the lines that work best.

Step 5: Write Down the References

- After the poem, list the Bible references for each verse in the order they appear. This lets others know where the verses are from.

Example: Creating a Poem on The Holy Ghost

1. Theme: Holy Ghost

2. Verses Found:
- John 14:26
"But the Advocate, the Holy Spirit, whom the Father will send in my name, will teach you all things and will remind you of everything I have said to you."

- Acts 1:8
"But you will receive power when the Holy Spirit comes on you; and you will be my witnesses in Jerusalem, and in all Judea and Samaria, and to the ends of the earth."

- Romans 8:26
"In the same way, the Spirit helps us in our weakness. We do not know what we ought to pray for, but the Spirit himself intercedes for us through wordless groans."

3. Arranged Poem:

The Advocate

"But the Advocate, the Holy Spirit,
 Whom the Father will send in my name,
 Will teach you all things
 And remind you of everything I have said to you."

"But you will receive power
 When the Holy Spirit comes on you;
 And you will be my witnesses—
 To the ends of the earth."

"In the same way, the Spirit helps us in our weakness.
 We do not know what we ought to pray for,
 But the Spirit himself intercedes for us
 Through wordless groans."

John 14:26; Acts 1:8; Romans 8:26

THAT'S IT!
You've created a Bible Verse Poem.

Glimpses of God

God, our foundation, through Christ, our salvation,

Opening our hearts to Faith beyond measure.

Overcoming Sin, we find Love everlasting,

Drawing near in Prayer, in Covenant treasure.

Trusting in Righteousness, Forgiveness sets free,

In Worship we rise, the Spirit our guide.

Miracles and Healing, His Grace multiplied,

Eternal Hope flows in life unified.

Steadfast in Justice, Mercy and Peace,

THROUGH GOOD TIMES IN HIM, OUR SOULS FIND RELEASE.

Copyright

ISBN 979-8-9893015-7-7

www.ingramcontent.com/pod-product-compliance
Lightning Source LLC
Chambersburg PA
CBHW030824090426
42737CB00009B/868